**Man was originally created
to live happily in God.**

So God created mankind in his own image,
in the image of God he created them; male and female he created them.
(Genesis 1:27)

**But man disobeyed and sinned against God,
thereby walking away from Him.**

Results = Anxiety + Fear + Death

For all have sinned and fall short of the glory of God (Romans 3:23)

For the wages of sin is death, but the gift of God is
eternal life in Christ Jesus our Lord. (Romans 6:23)

**God had mercy on sinful humanity and sent Jesus Christ
into the world as a ransom for us.**

Whoever does not love does not know God,
because God is Love (1John 4:8)

For even the Son of Man did not come to be served,
but to serve, and to give his life as a ransom for many. (Mark 10:45)

**Jesus died on the cross, and was buried,
but rose from the dead on the third day to pay for all of our sins.
Now, He wants us to have two gifts.**

Gifts = Peace + Eternal Life

Peace I leave with you; my peace I give you. I do not give to you as the
world gives. Do not let your hearts be troubled and
do not be afraid. (John 14:27)

The thief comes only to steal and kill and destroy; I have come that
they may have life, and have it to the full. (John 10:10)

Don't you want to enjoy peace and eternal life?

God wants you to accept Jesus Christ into your heart
so that you may receive the gift of eternal life
and live in true peace.

For God so loved the world that He
gave his one and only Son, that whoever believes in him shall not perish
but have eternal life. (John 3:16)

Yet to all who did receive him, to those who believed in his name,
He gave the right to become children of God (John 1:12)

**Jesus is knocking at the door of your heart at this moment.
Now you must make a decision. You could choose to live
with fear and anxiety in the midst of this sinful world
and be condemned to eternal separation from God,
or you could choose to enjoy true peace and eternal life with God.**

**Would you like to accept Jesus into your heart
as your Lord and Savior?**

Here I am! I stand at the door and knock. If anyone
hears my voice and opens the door, I will come in and eat with that person,
and they with me. (Revelation 3:20)

You have made a vitally important decision.
Please pray the following prayer:

Father God, I am a sinner in need of you.
Please forgive me of my sins as I repent before you.
I believe that Jesus died on the cross for me
and rose from the grave to pay for my sins
Please come into my heart as my Lord and Savior.
In Jesus' name I pray, Amen.

Now that you have received Jesus Christ into your heart,
you are a child of God.

Please visit a nearby Bible-based, Gospel-centered church,
and begin the wonderful journey in Christ.
May the Lord richly bless you with His love!